THEODORE E. STEINWAY

PEOPLE AND PIANOS

A CENTURY OF SERVICE TO MUSIC

STEINWAY & SONS NEW YORK 1853·1953

DEDICATORY PREFACE

ABOUT ONE HUNDRED YEARS AGO the Steinway family emigrated from their native land to the New World, seeking a haven, opportunity, and the right to life, liberty, and the pursuit of happiness.

On June 29, 1850, they arrived in New York City with eager heart and hopeful vision.

The City of New York held out its arms in welcome, gave them a new home, fresh hope, and the blessed privilege of doing their work, thinking their thoughts, and living their lives in peace, security, and service to music.

This book briefly tells the story of the Steinways' first hundred years—one small grain among the endless sands of time; but still their own.

In 1853 the House of Steinway was founded in New York City. In this year 1953, as a small token of an infinitely great debt, they humbly dedicate this book to the City of New York and its people.

Steinway Hall, New York, 1953

CONTENTS

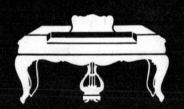

1836 · 1853 · 1866

ORIGINS

Brady, New York.

Henry Engelhard Steinway (1797-1871).

ORIGINS

An institution is the lengthened shadow of one man.

EMERSON

Henry Engelhard Steinway, small in physical stature but strong-willed, sturdy, and courageous, had already lived two-thirds of his life when he came to the United States in 1850. Behind him lay one career as a master cabinet maker and another as a master piano builder. Into his two remaining decades he crowded the achievement of a lifetime. Aided by his children, he contributed more than any other man to the development of piano making from a craft to an industry. That the craftsman's conscience was not lost in the transition from the family-staffed workshop to the factory manned by hundreds is his doing.

Heinrich Engelhard Steinweg, as he was then called, settled in 1820 in the little town of Seesen, in the Harz mountains of Central Germany. It was here that he married Juliane Thiemer and raised a family of five sons and three daughters. It was here, too, that his career as a piano maker began—with an instrument built, according to family tradition, in the kitchen of his Seesen house as a spare-time project in 1836.

The rewards of a growing but small business in a provincial German town were no match for the attraction America had for ambitious Germans of the 1840s. Even if there had been no revolution in 1848, the Steinways would probably have headed toward the New World in due course of time. But the ill-fated revolt had the effect of hastening their decision.

Henry's son Charles, a liberal who had been politically out of favor since his participation in that affair, immigrated to the United States in 1849—one of the large number of enterprising Germans of liberal turn of mind who made this move about that time. He got a job as a cabinet maker, and at his insistence the rest of the family soon followed. Only C. F. Theodore Steinway, the eldest son, stayed behind to run his own piano factory. The family arrived in New York on June 29, 1850, moved into a tenement at 199 Hester Street, and the men immediately took piano-building jobs wherever they could find them.

It was during the middle years of the nineteenth century that the piano became established in its permanent position in the eyes of the American public, both as a musical instrument and as a piece of furniture. Interest in music was growing fast, as evidenced by Jenny Lind's triumphant tour in 1850-1851, and more and more people could afford to indulge their tastes. More than ever in homes where music was loved, the piano was becoming a member of the family.

Its great range, virtually encompassing that of the human ear; its power and depth of tone; its versatility in tone color, shadings, and subtle nuances which composers indicate and musicians seek to interpret—all these establish the piano's basic position in music. It was during the nineteenth century, particularly, that the increasing complexity of the instrument and the broadening of its capabilities invited the composition of music which took advantage of this development; this in turn made further demands upon piano makers to keep pace. The Steinways were keenly aware of this demand.

Although business conditions in general were poor in the early days of their life in this country, none of the family was unemployed for very long. But other problems plagued them: the fast pace of work and the rigors of an unfamiliar climate. In 1852, discouraged and seriously weakened by constant overwork, Charles summed it up in a letter to Theodore in Germany: "Of course America is a haven for anyone willing to work, who had no employment in Germany and had to contend with hardships and worries; but nothing is perfect, not even human happiness in America. . . ."

In spite of discouragements and illness the family made progress in their trade, and in 1853 the firm of Steinway & Sons was formed as a verbal partnership. Operations were begun in a rented loft at 85 Varick Street, not far from the present entrance to the Holland Tunnel. Doretta, the eldest daughter, was the star salesman and sometimes offered to give free piano lessons to prospective buyers in order to close the sale. Within a year their rented loft space became inadequate, and the firm moved into larger quarters at 82-88 Walker Street. A photograph of the period shows the elegant clothes and fine carriages of the members of the firm—surely an indication of prosperity.

The Steinways were quick to adopt the overstrung scale, in which the strings are arranged radially in two layers, the treble below the bass, yielding greatly improved tone quality and power. The first of the many prizes awarded the firm was for overstrung square pianos with full iron frames, exhibited at the American Institute Fair in the New York Crystal Palace in 1855. In the disastrous fire that destroyed the Palace in 1858, they lost 17 fine instruments. Soon after this setback, however, Henry Steinway, Jr., was ready with his epoch-making invention: the application of the overstrung scale to grand pianos.

Unceasing experimentation and study lie behind the overstrung grand and the 18 other improvements patented by the Steinways during their first two decades as a firm. The correspondence between Henry Jr. in New York and his brother Theodore in Germany bristles with records of experiments, with diagrams and mechanical discussions. Henry combined technical inventiveness with an interest in marketing. It was probably his idea to promote piano sales through the endorsements of famous musicians, a policy that was to help make Steinway an international institution in later years. Theodore, a voluminous correspondent with an abominable handwriting, was a brilliant engineer and scientist. He later developed, partly on the groundwork laid by Henry, most of the major improvements associated with the firm's name.

Removal to Walker Street, 1854.

Gold Medal of the American Institute, 1855.

In the meantime, business boomed. Soon a new factory and lumber yard were going up on a truly large scale. The new plant was located far uptown, occupying the whole blockfront between 52nd and 53rd Streets on Fourth (now Park) Avenue and extending east to Lexington Avenue. It was opened in 1860 and remained in use until the gradual removal of operations to Long Island was completed in 1910. For the first time in the history of the firm power-driven woodworking machinery was installed—one of the earliest applications of mechanical power in the industry.

For all its size, however, the business had remained a family affair—a fact which found concrete expression in the three identical brownstone houses, adjoining the factory, which housed the boss and two of his sons with their families.

Though warerooms were temporarily set up in the factory, plans were already in the making for a combined salesroom and office building downtown. The firm planned also to build a concert hall, to stimulate popular interest in music and thus to increase the demand for pianos.

Before long, construction was going on from 14th Street to 15th Street, between Fourth Avenue and Irving Place—a more fashionable neighborhood at the time than it is now. Though the Civil War slowed down all building, the warerooms, offices, and studios were completed in 1864; the concert hall had to wait until the war was over.

The skills available in a piano factory could not in those days be diverted for military purposes, as they are in the mechanized warfare of our own time. In patriotic parades the House of Steinway was represented by nothing more martial than a piano on a horse-drawn truck draped with flags. But the Steinways, like so many who had emigrated from Germany, were strongly in sympathy with the cause of the Union. Charles volunteered at 32 and became paymaster of the 5th New York Regiment; Albert, at 21, was a second lieutenant in the same unit. Another serviceman was Theodore Vogel, husband of Wilhelmina Steinway and superintendent of the plant.

Steinway Hall, opened in 1866, almost immediately became an artistic and cultural center. It was not only the scene of concerts and lectures—civic and political meetings also were frequently held there. Among the latter, the National Woman Suffrage convention of 1872, for which the Reverend Henry Ward Beecher guaranteed the hall rent, was to become memorable. It was in an attempt to capture this meeting that the notorious Victoria Woodhull, spiritualist, quack healer, stockbroker, and advocate of free love, formed the Equal Rights party, on the ticket of which she ran for President later in the year.

The Civil War had taken no lives in the Steinway family, but the year 1865 was a disastrous one. Henry Jr., after years of suffering, succumbed to tuberculosis in early March, and before the month was over Charles had died of typhoid while visiting Theodore in Germany. This left Henry Engelhard, who was 68 years old, and young Albert and William with the staggering task of carrying on the business which had grown so rapidly. They took the only possible course: they asked Theodore to give up his business in Germany and to join them as a partner. Theodore arrived in New York on October 26, 1865.

Seesen, Germany, in the early nineteenth century; Henry
Engelhard Steinway's home from 1820 to 1850.

The Steinway house in Seesen, the birthplace of the second generation of Steinways.

The oldest known piano bearing a Steinway label, said to have been built in the kitchen of the Seesen house in 1836. Now in the possession of Steinway & Sons.

S. S. "Helene Sloman," on which the Steinways came to the United States in 1850.

Jenny Lind *(right)*, whose tour in 1850-1851 set a new high in American musical life. Her opening concert at Castle Garden *(left)* probably was the Steinway's first major musical experience in the New World.

Letter from Charles Steinway to his brother Theodore in Germany, 1852.

". . . I cannot advise you to come here if you are able, by diligence and thrift, to make a living in Germany . . . People here have to work harder than abroad, and you get so used to better living that you finally think potato soup tasted better in Germany than the daily roast here . . . The worst thing for the Germans is that few of them can stand the climate; almost all have chest pains..."

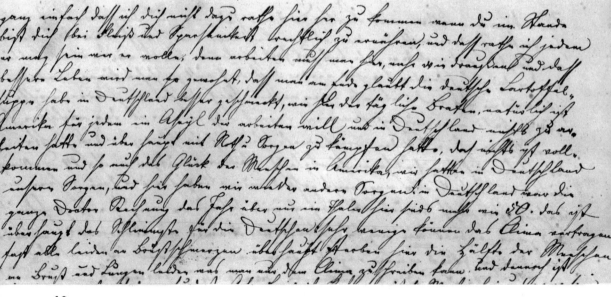

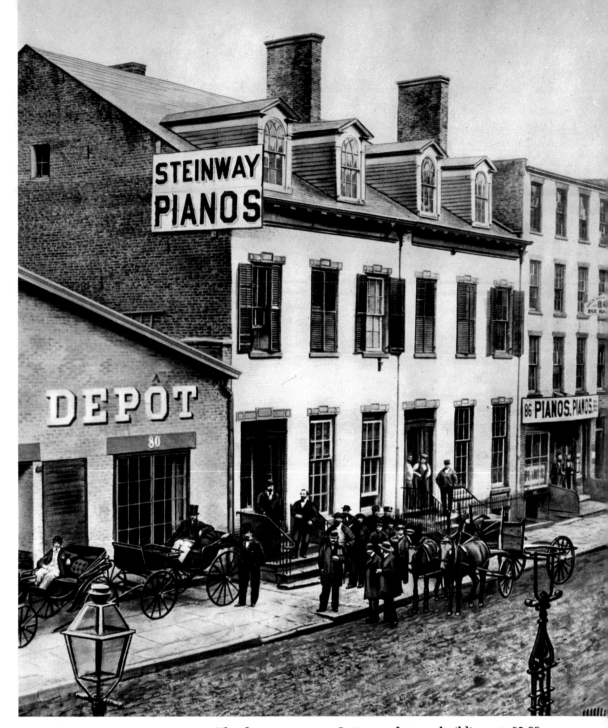

The first permanent Steinway factory building, at 82-88 Walker Street, New York City; occupied from 1854 to 1860. The building at No. 82 is still standing. The entire family and staff are assembled in front.

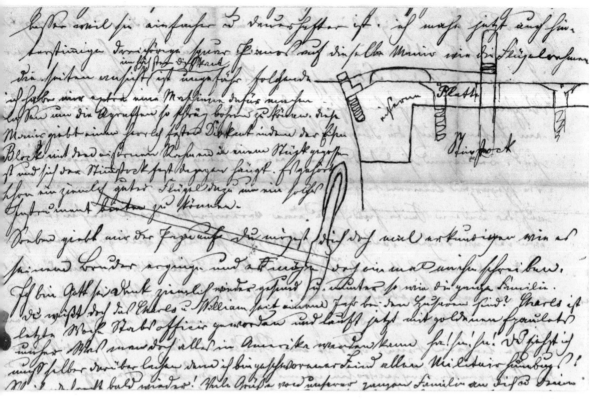

Letter from Henry Steinway, Jr., to C. F. Theodore Steinway, 1859: description of pinblock assembly with flanged plate, one of the basic Steinway developments.

"The cross section in the highest treble looks about like this. I have had a machine specially made in order to drill the agraffes diagonally. This method provides a beautifully firm mounting in the treble, in that the bar is cast in one piece with the frame, and the pinblock is firmly lodged against it. It takes a pretty good grand to beat such an instrument."

The flange of the frame *(upper left in diagram)*, fitted solidly to the pinblock *(right)*, permits greatly increased string tension and consequently improved tone quality.

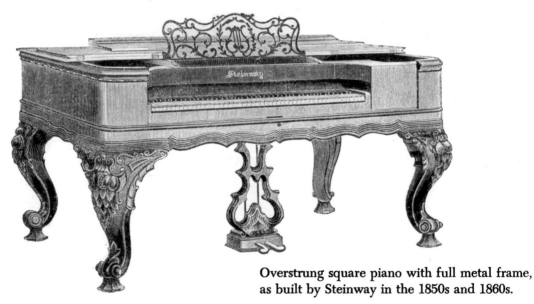

Overstrung square piano with full metal frame, as built by Steinway in the 1850s and 1860s.

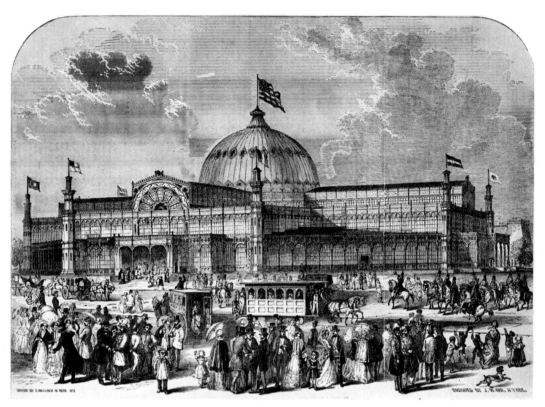

Crystal Palace, New York City, where the Steinways exhibited their square pianos and first received a prize, the gold medal of the American Institute, in 1855.

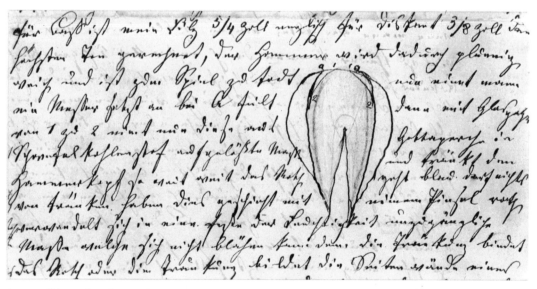

Letter from Theodore, about 1859, on a new method for treating hammer heads.

"Take a solution of gutta-percha in carbon disulphide and drench the hammer head with it as far as the red area goes" (i.e., the sides of the hammer). The material then "changes into a solid mass, impervious to moisture, which cannot swell." The innovation was not successful.

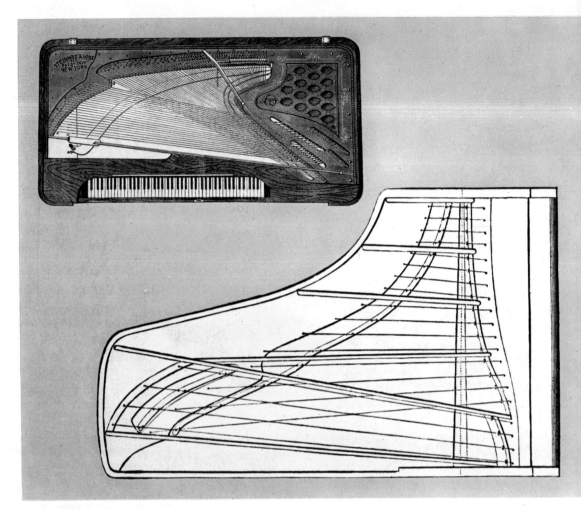

The first great Steinway invention: the overstrung grand. Previously used in square pianos by many makers *(above left)*, overstringing was applied to the grand piano *(below)* by Henry Steinway, Jr., in 1859.

Henry Steinway, Jr. (1831-1865).

Advertisement for overstrung square and grand pianos, 1860. This is an early example of the use in advertising of endorsements by prominent musicians.

STEINWAY & SONS'

Patent Overstrung Grand and Square Pianos

Are now considered the best Pianos manufactured.

OPINION OF NEARLY ALL THE GREATEST AND MOST PROMINENT MUSICIANS AND ARTISTS REGARDING THESE INSTRUMENTS:

The undersigned having personally examined and practically tested the improvement in Grand Pianos, invented by H. STEINWAY, in which the covered strings are overstrung above those remaining, do hereby certify:

1. That as a result of the said improvement the voice of the Piano is greatly improved in quality, quantity and power.

2. The sound by Steinway's improvement is much more even, less harsh, stronger, and much better prolonged than that realized in any other Piano with which we are acquainted.

3. The undersigned regard the improvement of Mr. Steinway as most novel, ingenious and important. No Piano of similar construction has ever been known or used, so far as the undersigned know or believe:

GUSTAV SATTER,	WILLIAM MASON,
S. B. MILLS,	JOHN N. PATTISON,
WM. SAAR,	ROBERT GOLDBECK,
U. C. HILL,	GEORGE W. MORGAN,
WM. A. KING,	CARL BERGMANN,
GEO. F. BRISTOW,	HENRY C. TIMM,

And many others.

Each Instrument warranted for the term of three years. Warerooms, 82 and 84 Walker St., near Broadway, New York   0000

Henry Jr. to Theodore, 1859: plans for further use of musicians' endorsements. This thought later matured into the Steinways' activity as artists' managers.

"Our overstrung grands are really excellent . . . If you read the musical journals, you will soon see a rave article about us and our business in the *Berliner Musikzeitung* and the *Leipziger Signale*. We are now anxious to make our name well known in Europe; this is absolutely necessary in order to interest those piano virtuosi who come here, so we'll get our hands on them . . ."

Factory on Park Avenue, between 52nd and 53rd Streets,
New York City. In use from 1860 until 1910. The New York
and Harlem Railroad, not yet lowered and covered over,
appears in the foreground.

Steinway homes at 121-125 East 52nd Street, adjoining the
factory. Henry Engelhard's house at the left, followed by
those of Henry Jr. and William.

Demonstration of pianos and banquet at the opening reception at the 53rd Street factory, 1860.

Sawing and planing room at the 53rd Street factory. Line-shaft-driven power tools are the earliest instance of mechanization in the Steinways' history.

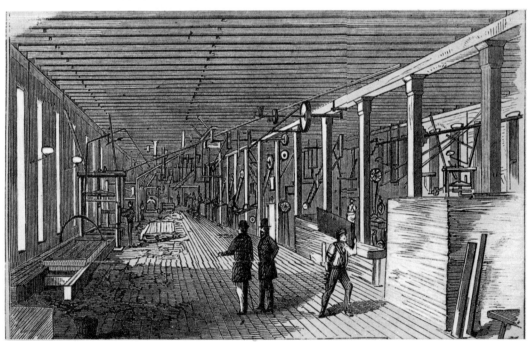

Steinway Hall, 71-73 (later renumbered 109-111) East 14th Street,
New York. The main office and sales rooms were here from 1864
until 1925. The concert hall was opened in 1866, closed in 1890.

Steinways and their kin in the Civil War. *Left to right:* Paymaster
Charles Steinway; Lt. Albert Steinway; Lt. Theodore Vogel.

Lt. Albert Steinway *(foreground)* and part of Company B,
5th New York Regiment, 1863.

Display in 1865 inaugural procession.

Above: Literature at Steinway Hall: ticket queue for reading by Charles Dickens, 1867. *Below:* Concert of the Vienna Lady Orchestra at Steinway Hall, 1871. The hall was one of New York's musical and cultural centers from 1866 until 1890.

Politics at Steinway Hall: communist
demonstrators ejected from a civic re-
form meeting, 1877.

Science at Steinway Hall: first demonstration of music
transmitted by wire (from Philadelphia to New York), 1877.

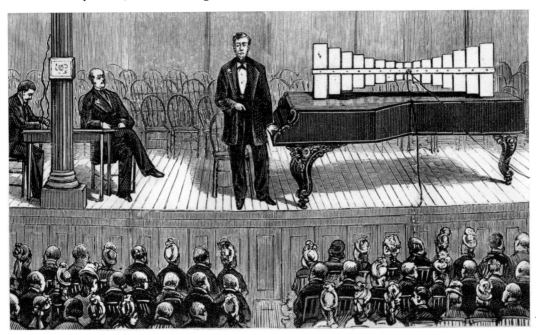

Sales room at Steinway Hall on 14th Street, 1864.

Above: Signatures on partnership agreement of 1861. *Below:* Partnership of 1866, drawn up after the deaths of Charles and Henry Jr. and the arrival of Theodore Steinway. By 1866 the Americanized form of the name, long used in nonlegal business, had become official.

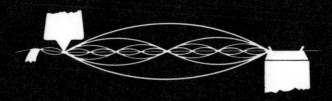

1866 · 1896

THE PERFECTION OF THE INSTRUMENT

Steinway grand specially designed to be shown at the Philadelphia Centennial Exhibition, 1876. The most elaborate Steinway piano built up to that date.

THE PERFECTION OF THE INSTRUMENT

Geselle ist, wer was kann;
Meister ist, wer was ersann;
Lehrling ist jedermann.

Who knows his trade is a journeyman;
A master is he that invents the plan;
An apprentice, each and every man.

MOTTO OF C. F. THEODORE STEINWAY

Henry Engelhard Steinway died in 1871. He had lived to see the growth of the company from the small workshop on Varick Street to the large complex factory on Fourth Avenue, the direction of which his sons Theodore, William, and Albert now took over.

Largely as a result of young Henry Steinway's inventions, the American grand piano had become established as a distinct type by the late 1860s. Within a few years, more new departures were made.

On the technical side, under the guidance of Theodore Steinway, assisted by Albert until the death of the latter in 1877, the pace of invention was tremendously accelerated: before the end of the century the Steinway grand was substantially the instrument we know today, and the upright had become the universal home piano.

On the artistic and cultural side there was Steinway Hall, where concerts by famous musicians were sponsored by the firm. It was also during the last three decades of the century that the family, mainly through

William Steinway, the president of the firm, took part most actively in New York civic affairs and in politics.

During this period, two strong figures of the House of Steinway stand out sharply. Temperamentally, they were as different as brothers could possibly be; yet each of them made contributions which were vital to the future of the firm.

Brilliant, irascible, meticulous Theodore Steinway, who now assumed supervision of the technical side of piano making, was a perfectionist in his attention to mechanical detail. More important, he was a trained engineer and scientist—perhaps the first in an industry that had until then relied more on hit-or-miss procedures than on systematic research. Although he built largely on the work of his late brother, young Henry, he quickened the pace of invention, research, and development; in fact he was himself responsible for 45 of the firm's 101 patents.

Theodore's success with upright pianos in Germany encouraged him to persist with their large-scale production here and enabled him to overcome the objection to them which had been voiced not only by the general public but even by his own workmen. Also, around 1880, after prolonged study of the steel industry both in the United States and in Europe, he succeeded in producing a cast frame which permitted string tension to be nearly doubled. As an experiment, he then built a parlor grand only six feet long, which had the same power and tone as those of much larger instruments.

Unlike his predecessors and most of his contemporaries, Theodore leaned heavily on theoretical research in acoustics. In this field he had the benefit of the advice and collaboration of Hermann von Helmholtz, the famous Berlin physicist, who enunciated the modern theory of overtones. The last of the family to come to the United States, Theodore, perhaps because he had no children, was least influenced by his foster land, although he did serve occasionally on civic committees. He always preferred life in Germany and returned to make his home in Brunswick after his retirement.

William Steinway had adapted himself quickly and thoroughly to life in the United States. He was urbane, warm-hearted; a man of imagination and broad interests in charitable and civic efforts as well as in business matters. (He once raised $112,000 for the German, now Lenox Hill, Hospital and was a liberal supporter of Abbey, Schoeffel & Grau, the managers of the Metropolitan Opera House.) In addition to presiding over Steinway & Sons from its incorporation in 1876 until 1896, William set up a land company, a streetcar line, and a ferry in connection with the firm's Long Island operations. He also had a hand in the East River Gas Company of Long Island City, and two banks counted him among their board members. About 1888 he entered into a partnership with Gottlieb Daimler and formed the Daimler Motor Company, which for a num-

Steinway post-office cancellation, 1888.

ber of years built stationary internal combustion engines and motors for cars and boats in a shop located at Steinway. The partnership, however, was not a comfortable one; when Daimler came for a visit in 1893, William confided to his diary: "Old Daimler [he was all of two years older than William] calls again nearly drives me to despair with his Ideas."

William Steinway played an active part in Democratic politics and was a lifelong friend of Grover Cleveland, to whom he made a personal gift of a piano upon the occasion of his wedding in the White House in 1886. He attended the Democratic convention of 1888 as a delegate, and in January, 1893, following Cleveland's second election, he braved the pains of a gouty knee to preside over the Presidential electors of the State of New York.

Public transportation claimed much of his attention. He was the original promoter of the East River tunnel between East 42nd Street, Manhattan, and Vernon Boulevard, Long Island City, now used by the IRT subway. He also served a fruitful term as chairman of the Rapid Transit Commission, which drew up the plans for the first subway in New York. William did not live to see the beginning of actual construction in 1900, but in 1933 a subway station perpetuating his name and that of the community he built was opened at Steinway Street and Broadway, Long Island City.

The story of this community begins in 1870 and 1871, when the firm, partly as an investment, partly for expansion, bought a 400-acre tract of farm land in what soon afterward became the northern end of Long Island City (itself now a part of New York City). In 1871 the lumber mill and foundry were established at the new location, in the western part of the present Riker Avenue plant. It was here that a model village named Steinway was built by the firm for its employees. This was the company's answer —an enlightened one by the standards of the period—to the radical labor agitation that had interfered with their work in the city. In later years, as social concepts changed, most of this real estate was sold, but the name still appears throughout the district—in the name of the principal thoroughfare, the bus line, and various stores and shops.

During its first few decades the village of Steinway was in effect a self-contained unit, with its own post office. The municipality of Long Island City, of which it was a part, existed mostly on paper, and public services rendered by the city were inadequate. To supplement them the family built a public bath, a park, and a library and kindergarten and organized a volunteer fire department They also subsidized the public school for the teaching of music and of German, which was for many years the everyday language in the factory.

All this building would not have been possible without the company's prosperity, which depended on the continuing demand for fine pianos. After the Paris exhibition of 1867 American pianos, as typified by the Steinway, had become popular in Europe almost overnight. Facing stiff competition from European manufacturers at first, the Steinway had found champions in Hector Berlioz and in the illustrator Gustave Doré, who was not only a social lion but also an accomplished amateur musician and who, by his endorsement, made it *de rigueur* in French society and thereby in all Europe. By 1877 a European sales office and service unit had become a necessity, and the London branch was established; a few years later, seven of every ten American pianos sold in Europe were Steinways. A branch factory was opened in Hamburg in 1880.

For the Philadelphia Centennial Exhibition in 1876 the Steinways designed their most elaborate instrument to date. At this time they acquired, in addition to the usual medal for excellence, a valuable staff member in the person of Nahum Stetson, who was serving as manager of the machinery exhibits at the fair and whom they hired as a sales representative as soon as the fair closed. They were motivated in this not only by Stetson's obvious ability but also by the realization that the company could use some native American talent—a need which Stetson, a Yankee from East Bridgewater, Massachusetts, was admirably equipped to

Charles Herman Steinway's season ticket for the Philadelphia Centennial Exhibition of 1876.

33

fill. Advanced later to the post of sales manager, he remained with the company until his retirement in 1930.

As a solo instrument, whether in the home or on the concert stage, the piano has brought to a music-hungry world the great masterworks of all time. Accompanied by an orchestra or as part of one, it adds its own brilliance and tone to the other voices around it. The piano serves, too, to accompany the human voice, as well as other musical instruments, complementing them and rounding out the individual performance. Through their close connection with great artists of the period and their sponsorship, at Steinway Hall, of concerts by noted musicians, the Steinways in these years demonstrated dramatically the range and scope of the piano's use.

When Henry Steinway, Jr., back in 1859, was thinking of sponsoring concert artists, he felt that the excellence of the instrument would be evident to the most critical of critics and that their enthusiastic acceptance of it would give it increased value in the public eye. These plans eventually took shape in the form of the Steinway Hall concerts, which combined publicity value for the firm

with a tangible service to music and musicians. To ensure quality in the concerts, the firm operated, and most successfully, as artists' managers.

In 1864 there had been some correspondence with Hans von Bülow on the possibility of an American tour, but nothing came of it. In 1872 Anton Rubinstein agreed to visit the United States under Steinway auspices. Since Rubinstein had some highly colored notions about life in America, the transaction was not without its funny side. He was careful to specify, for example, that he could not be required to play in beer gardens. He trusted neither greenbacks nor banks; at the end of his tour he is said to have insisted on a settlement in gold until he was invited to lift a bag of gold coins in the amount of 200,000 French francs, weighing about 140 pounds. But his strenuous and highly successful tour of 215 concerts all over the country, with the violinist Henri Wieniawski, set a pattern for future ventures of this sort. In a later generation Rubinstein's pupil Josef Hofmann was to become one of the great artists who played the Steinway piano.

Steinway Hall closed its doors in 1890 and was superseded by Carnegie Hall as the city's principal concert auditorium. But at the opening series of concerts at the latter hall in 1891 the Steinway was the instrument on which Adele aus der Ohe played Tchaikovsky's B-flat minor concerto, with the composer himself conducting. Later in the year at Carnegie Hall the Steinways as concert managers presented Ignace Jan Paderewski to his first American audience, with considerable fanfare. A spectacular success even in the advance sales, Paderewski's first tour netted some $15,000 over the preliminary estimates, but the firm refused to accept the sum. A few years later, with part of the proceeds of his tours, Paderewski established a trust fund for American musicians, of which William Steinway, just before his death, became a charter trustee.

Amusements.

IGNACE J. PADEREWSKI'S

INAUGURAL CONCERTS,

WITH ORCHESTRA,

WALTER DAMROSCH, Conductor,

will take place at

NEW MUSIC HALL on

Tuesday Evening, Nov. 17, at 8:15.

Thursday Evening, Nov. 19, at 8:15.

Saturday Afternoon, Nov. 21, at 2:30.

RESERVED SEATS, $2, $1.50, ALSO $1,

ACCORDING TO LOCATION.

——SPECIAL NOTICE.——

OWING TO THE EXTRAORDINARY DEMAND FOR RESERVED SEATS IT HAS BEEN DECIDED TO RESERVE THE ENTIRE BALCONY FOR THE FIRST CONCERT (ONLY) AT ONE (1) DOLLAR EACH, TICKETS FOR WHICH CAN NOW BE HAD AT THE BOX OFFICE, MUSIC HALL, 57TH ST. AND 7TH AV., AND AT EDWARD SCHUBERTH & CO.'S, 23 UNION SQUARE.

STEINWAY & SONS' PIANOS USED.

Paderewski's American première, 1891.

C. F. Theodore Steinway (1825-1889), head of the technical departments of Steinway & Sons from 1865, was largely responsible for the synthesis of the modern piano, basing his work on current research in acoustics.

Double cupola iron frame, invented by Theodore Steinway in 1872. The frame, cast in one piece, increases in height from the keyboard backward, leaving room under its rear portion to permit the use, in large grands, of the continuous soundboard bridge (zigzag pattern in diagram).

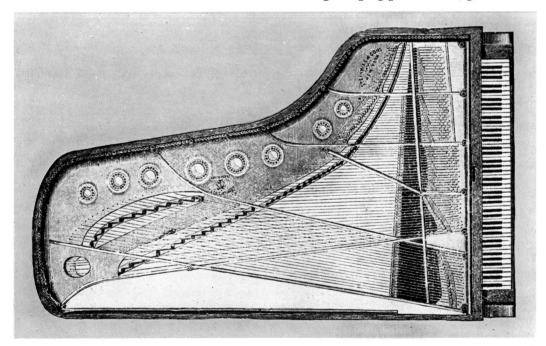

Hermann von Helmholtz (1821-1894), the great physicist. He corresponded with the Steinways about piano acoustics from the early 1870s until his death.

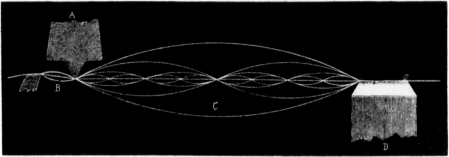

Principle of the duplex scale, invented by Theodore Steinway on the basis of Helmholtz's researches, 1872.

Each string has, beside its main section (C), a proportionate extra length (B) which vibrates in harmony with the main section, increasing the richness of the tone.

Typical Steinway upright of the 1880s. Large-scale manufacture of uprights began in the early 1870s, at Theodore Steinway's suggestion.

Piano rims are still formed according to Theodore Steinway's method *(above)*. As many as 22 layers of wood are
glued together and bent into shape in a steel press before
the glue sets. A screw clamp Theodore invented for the
purpose was patented in 1880 *(below)*.

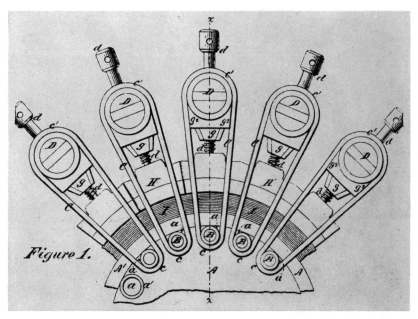

Figure 1.

The scale-drawing room at the 53rd Street factory, Theodore Steinway's work room.

The Committee of Seventy investigation of the Tweed Ring, 1871. Cartoon by Thomas Nast. Theodore Steinway served on this committee, which probed the most scandalous corruption in the history of New York.

NEXT!

William Steinway (1836-1896), head of
the firm from 1876 until his death.

Entry in William Steinway's diary, recording his chairmanship of the
New York electors in the 1892 election, which returned his friend Grover
Cleveland to the White House. The "Murphy resolution" was a highly
irregular maneuver by which the Democratic machine obtained an endorsement by the electors of the Senatorial candidacy of Edward Murphy.

Above: Plan for a local subway station under Broadway, drawn up by the New York City Rapid Transit Commission under William Steinway, 1891. *Below:* William Steinway's name commemorated in a subway station in Long Island City, built in 1933.

Ferryboat "Steinway" of the 92nd Street-Astoria ferry line, one of William Steinway's side ventures.

Daimler Motor Victoria, built in Germany for the Chicago World's Fair of 1893 to publicize William Steinway's [American] Daimler Motor Company.

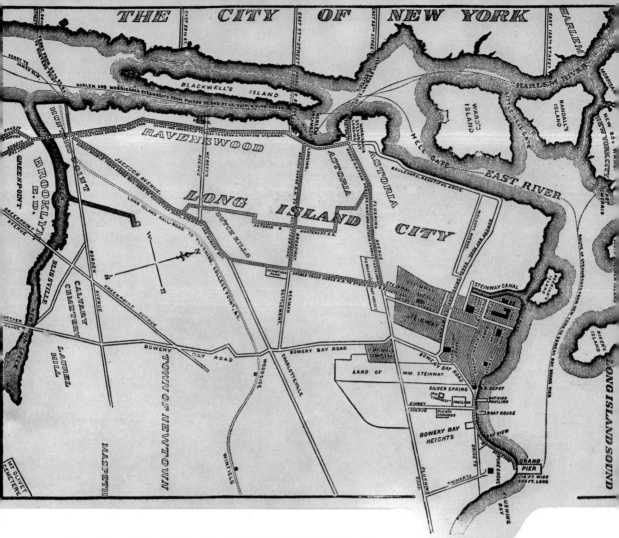

Above: Long Island City, New York, in the 1880s, showing the Steinway landholdings (shaded area). *Below:* Mementoes of Old Steinway Village, Long Island City, 1953. The neighborhood is still unofficially known as "Steinway."

Riker Avenue factory at Steinway Village *(above)*, opened
1871, views about 1880. The plant, consisting of lumber
yard, sawmill, casemaking shop, and foundry, was built on
the water's edge, where lumber could be floated in *(below)*
and foundry sand and pig iron delivered on barges.

Steinway Mansion, the summer home of the Steinway family in the late nineteenth century. Sold later, it is still standing east of Steinway Street (formerly Steinway Avenue) near the river.

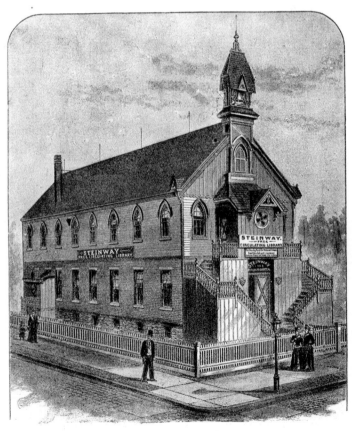

Steinway Free Library and Kindergarten, 1896. One of many public benefits provided by Steinway & Sons for their employees.

Steinway volunteer fire department in the 1870s, before adequate facilities were provided by the Long Island City municipality.

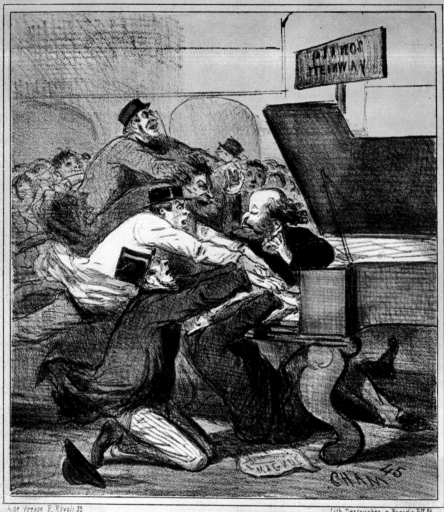

Le public de l'exposition, saisit tout à coup de la rage de se faire pianiste à l'audition des admirables pianos américains Steinway.

To Mr. Theodore E. Steinway, beloved President of "my dear and inseparable Friend, the Steinway Piano" From his devoted young friend
W. Horowitz
New-York

A V. Horowitz
En souvenir de la belle visite
du 6 Mars 1926

By 1867, the American piano had become a distinct type. The Paris exposition of that year suddenly popularized Steinway in Europe. Lithograph by Amédée de Noé ("Cham"). The pianist is Desiré Magnus.

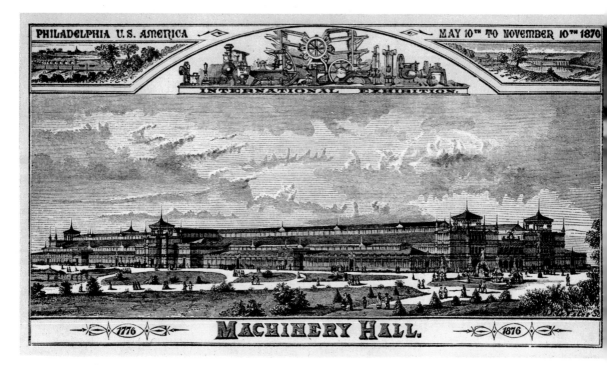

Steinway at the Centennial Exhibition, Philadelphia, 1876. *Above:* Machinery Hall where—incongruously enough—all music exhibits were displayed. *Below, right:* The Steinway exhibit.

Nahum Stetson, manager of the Machinery Hall exhibits in 1876; sales representative and later sales manager of Steinway & Sons, 1876-1930.

47

London sales office, 15-17, Lower Seymour Street (later Wigmore Street), W.1, opened in 1877 to handle the increasing export of Steinway pianos all over the world. A concert hall was built in the rear.

Steinway factory in Hamburg, Neue Rosenstrasse (later Schanzenstrasse) 20-24, with residence of the manager. Opened in 1880 to supply pianos for the European and other export markets. Totally destroyed in 1943.

Richard Wagner at his Steinway. Painted by Harry Townsend for the Steinway Collection. The firm presented this grand piano to Wagner on the occasion of the first Bayreuth opening in 1876.

Note by Wagner to Steinway's Hanover agent, concerning a piano loaned to him during a concert tour in 1875.

"Sincere thanks for the incomparably beautiful Steinway Grand, which certainly is worthy of a better piano player than, yours gratefully, RICHARD WAGNER."

Left: Franz Liszt in 1884, from a photograph in the possession of Steinway & Sons. *Right:* Letter from Liszt, 1884.

"When Mr. Steinway gets here, I shall have a piano shop talk with him, about the new construction of his grands. F. LISZT."

Above: Thomas A. Edison with his phonograph, 1888.
Below: Edison's purchase order for a Steinway, 1890.

From the Laboratory
of
Thomas A. Edison.

Orange, N.J. June 2nd 90 —

Steinway & Sons.
        Gents.

I have decided to keep your grand piano,
For some reason unknown to me it gives
better results than any so far tried.
Please send bill with lowest price

                Yours

                Thomas A Edison

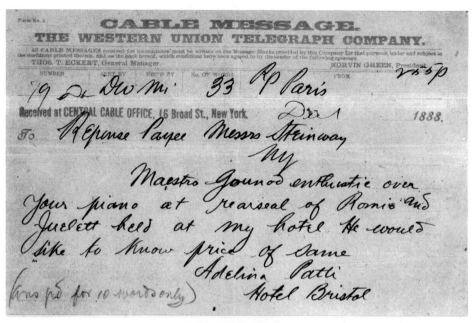

CABLE MESSAGE.
THE WESTERN UNION TELEGRAPH COMPANY.

All CABLE MESSAGES received for transmission must be written on the Message Blanks provided by this Company for that purpose, under and subject to the conditions printed thereon, and on the back hereof, which conditions have been agreed to by the sender of the following message.
THOS. T. ECKERT, General Manager.   NORVIN GREEN, President.

NUMBER   SENT BY   REC'D BY   No. Of WORDS   FROM

19   Dr   Dro Mi   33   Pp Paris

Received at CENTRAL CABLE OFFICE, 16 Broad St., New York.   Dec 1   1888.

To   Réponse Payee Messrs Steinway
NY

Maestro Gounod enthusiastic over your piano at rearseal of Romio and Juelett held at my hotel He would like to know price of same
Adelina Patti
Hotel Bristol

(ans pd for 10 words only)

The following message is received via French Cable at 1020u M. subject to the terms and conditions printed on the back hereof which are ratified and agreed to.

No. of Words   9
From Paris   To Steinway
facteur Pianos
ny

Mille graces lettre suit

Gounod

Sale of a Steinway piano to Charles Gounod through the good offices of Adelina Patti, 1888.

52

The first major artist brought to the United States by Steinway & Sons: Anton Rubinstein, who toured the country in 1872-1873.

Portion of contract between Steinway & Sons and Rubinstein. Maurice Grau was Rubinstein's manager.

"Mr. Rubinstein furthermore is not obliged . . . to play in establishments devoted to purposes other than artistic ones (at garden concerts, tobacco establishments [i.e. cafes], etc.)."

Caricature of Rubinstein concerts at Steinway Hall, 1872, by Joseph Keppler. Theodore Thomas in the upper left. Carlotta Patti second from left. Rubinstein at the piano. At right: Henri Wieniawski; Clara Louise Kellogg, at end of stage. Keppler himself at lower right, holding top hat.

Rubinstein later became the teacher of another great Steinway pianist, Josef Hofmann. Painting by Charles E. Chambers, in the Steinway collection.

American debut of Fritz Kreisler, at the age of 13, playing the Mendelssohn concerto at Steinway Hall in 1888. Anton Seidl (*right*) was the conductor.

THE
STEINWAY HALL
PROGRAMME.

NEW YORK, SATURDAY, NOVEMBER 10TH, 1888.

ANTON SEIDL'S
GRAND ORCHESTRAL CONCERTS.

FIRST SUBSCRIPTION CONCERT,
SATURDAY EVENING, NOVEMBER 10th, 1888,
AT 8.15 PRECISELY.

Soloists:

MR. CONRAD ANSORGE, PIANIST.

MASTER FRITZ KREISLER, VIOLINIST.

His first appearance in N. Y., by kind permission of Mr. EDMUND C. STANTON, Director Metropolitan Opera Co.

PROGRAMME.

1. SYMPHONY PASTORALE—No. 6, in F, Opus 68, ... LUDWIG VAN BEETHOVEN
   a, *Allegro ma non troppo.*
      Erwachen heiterer Empfindungen bei der Ankunft auf dem Lande.—The cheerful impressions excited on arriving in the Country.
   b, *Andante molto moto.*
      Scene am Bach.—Scene by the Brook.
   c, *Allegro.*
      Lustiges Zusammensein der Landleute.—Peasants merry-making.
      Allegro. Gewitter-Sturm.—Storm.
      Allegretto. { Hirtengesang; frohe und dankbare Gefühle nach dem Sturm.
                    { The shepherd's song; glad and thankful greetings after the storm.

2. WANDERER-FANTASIA, ... FRANZ SCHUBERT
   (Arranged with Orchestra by FRANZ LISZT.)
   a, Allegro con fuoco ma non troppo. b, Adagio. c, Presto. d, Allegro.
   Mr. CONRAD ANSORGE.

3. ENTREACT—*The Three Pintos,** (first time,) . . . . CARL MARIA VON WEBER

4. CONCERTO FOR VIOLIN in E minor, ... FELIX MENDELSSOHN-BARTHOLDI
   a, Allegro molto appassionato. b, Andante. Allegro molto vivace.
   Master FRITZ KREISLER.

5. "THE BIRD SERMON OF SAINT FRANCIS OF ASSISI"—Legend * . . . . FRANZ LISZT

A few of the noted pianists who played the Steinway. *Left to right*: Annette Essipova, Teresa Carreño (on a stamp of her native Venezuela), Raffael Joseffy.

Composers, conductors, and educators used and often bought Steinway pianos, among them *(left to right)*: Edward MacDowell, Arthur Nikisch, Alexander Lambert.

The Theodore Thomas orchestra at Steinway Hall, during the hall's last season, 1890.

Charles F. Tretbar, concert manager during the period when Steinway & Sons operated as artists' agents (about 1870-1900).

Steinway Hall closed in 1890, to be superseded by Carnegie Hall. During the series of opening concerts at the latter, Adele aus der Ohe (*below, right*) played Tchaikovsky's B-flat minor concerto on a Steinway, with the composer (*left*) conducting.

Steinway
Th. Wüst
An ad. of 1000 words could not be more eloquent than

PADEREWSKI AT HIS FAVORITE PIANO.

The year 1891 brought the first of Paderewski's triumphs in the United States, under Steinway management *(right)*. The portrait, inscribed by Paderewski, is dated from 1896.

To come to Hecuba without further parley, let us say that Mr. Paderewski, who effected an entrance on the American concert stage last night in the Music Hall, was dangerously well advertised.

Had he failed to satisfy the expectations which had been aroused among the musically inclined people of New-York his failure would have been nothing short of disastrous to his future in this country and a woful humiliation to his manager. Both were brilliantly rescued by his marvellous achievements. Nobody, not even the most diplomatic of the newspaper reviewers in this city, who have most need of conservatism, can have left the Music Hall last night without carrying with him a most decided conviction touching his thoughts about the much heralded newcomer. It was a case in which Caesar's boastful motto would have sounded like an expression of modest self-respect in the mouth of the pianist. He came, he saw, he conquered.

friends. We cannot but admire the fullness and strength of its tone as well as the mildness and softness of the same, qualities which one rarely finds united. The instrument found the same degree of applause and admiration, also among

my friends, who tried it. One of them, my colleague Professor Planck is a very skilful musician, and at the same time a first rate mathematician and physicist. He is my successor at the Berlin University in teaching the acoustical theory of Music. To his judgment I have the greatest confidence and he was quite of the same opinion as my other friends, my wife and myself. We feel us, therefore,

Dr. H. v. Helmholtz

Letter from Helmholtz, with thanks for a piano presented to him while visiting the New York factory in 1893. "Professor Planck" is Max Planck, the author of the quantum theory of thermodynamics.

1896 · 1953

THE INSTRUMENT OF THE IMMORTALS

Ignace Jan Paderewski. Painted by Ignacio
Zuloaga for the Steinway Collection.

THE INSTRUMENT OF THE IMMORTALS

Trifles make perfection, and perfection is no trifle.

MICHELANGELO

If companies, like people, can be said to reach maturity at a certain age, Steinway & Sons attained theirs about the turn of the century. Over the roughly five decades prior to 1900 their engineers had created a new kind of piano which by this time was accepted as the standard piano of the world. The efforts of their successors were to be directed toward refining the instrument and developing pianos suitable for the small home or apartment. Although the progress of piano making in the first half of this century was steady and patient, the growth in the dissemination and appreciation of music in America was almost explosive. To this growth the family and the firm contributed both directly and indirectly.

The tide of prosperity in the early years of the century brought with it an increasing preoccupation with culture—a sort of compulsion toward the arts. In the houses of the rich the custom-made piano was one of the visible symbols of this preoccupation. The Steinways, already recognized as makers of the finest pianos, built large numbers of elaborate and ornate cases around the standard insides. Orders and royal appointments came to them from heads of state all over the world. In 1903 they built piano number 100,000 for the White House. Yet not all of

their efforts went into large, luxurious pianos. In the privacy of the scale room Henry Ziegler, grandson of the founder, following a course pointed out by Theodore 25 years earlier, was laying plans for grands and uprights smaller than any previously built, long before the need for such instruments was generally recognized.

It was an age of concert triumphs, too, and Steinway & Sons, the makers of what came to be called "the Instrument of the Immortals," had a share in them. Paderewski was now at the height of his fame. Though the firm, in keeping with the growing specialization in the field of music, had gradually given up artist management, it expanded its services as suppliers of concert and rehearsal instruments to scores of artists. That relationship often ripened into cordial friendship; the Steinway round table at Lüchow's restaurant on 14th Street became a meeting place for musicians from all over the world.

Public recognition became more widespread, and before long operations had to be rescaled to cope with the growing demand for Steinway pianos. Charles H. Steinway, William's successor as president, and his sales manager Ernest Urchs tried to set up a chain of branch stores in the larger cities. It soon became apparent, however, that pianos could be sold as well or better through dealers, and through them Steinway's concert and repair services blanketed most of the United States. About the same time the Long Island factories were enlarged to substantially their present size, and a large addition was built in Hamburg.

The expansion of operations had no effect on the traditional standards of workmanship, however. New materials and methods of manufacture were under constant study. Minor improvements and refinements were made from time to time. Machine work was substituted for hand work only in the relatively few operations where quality would not be affected in the slightest—a policy which has never been modified. Even so, the power-driven tool must still be guided by the hand of man.

The First World War took 63 men, including two Steinway descendants of the fourth American generation, away from their jobs. The restless postwar years brought some unexpected developments to music and musicians. Rachmaninoff and Alexander Siloti, both of whom were to become firm friends of the House of Steinway, came to the United States as refugees from the Russian Revolution. Paderewski, long noted as a Polish patriot, entered politics in 1919 and served as the first premier of the new Polish republic. Some of the pianos the Steinways built suffered strange fates, too. In Istanbul the new Turkish government found among the deposed Sultan's effects a substantial number of pianos which had been bought for the ladies of the imperial harem about 1908 and which had never been uncrated.

By 1921, before Europe was fully settled down, the firm resumed its expansion program. While Germany was heading into the inflation that was to bankrupt the country, a whole new factory, the Rondenbarg plant, was built on the western outskirts of Hamburg. In 1925 the London office was moved into larger quarters. In the same year, after a

Paderewski stamp of Poland, autographed by him for Theodore E. Steinway.

decade of planning, the present Steinway Hall was completed at 109 West 57th Street in New York. Finally, an additional factory building was put up on Long Island.

Meanwhile, technical developments in the field of music were to have a profound effect upon piano making. By the early 1920s the mechanical reproduction of sound made good music available to tremendous numbers of people who had never enjoyed it before. The player piano reached the peak of its popularity about 1924, with noted pianists like Josef Hofmann making player roll recordings. Although the Steinways never took up the manufacture of player pianos, they did build instruments which could house the Duo-Art player mechanism, which was made and installed by the Aeolian Company of America. At the same time a large body of music on phonograph records (still imperfect owing to early recording techniques) was coming into being. And in 1922 for the first time a Steinway piano was sold to a radio station—WJZ, then operated by the Westinghouse Company in Newark, New Jersey. In the early days of radio, pianos had to be "voiced down" so as not to drown out the other performers.

The "Steinway artists" of the period are legion; letters of commendation came in from Olga Samaroff, Leopold Auer, George Gershwin, Ignaz Friedman, Frederick Stock, Bronislaw Hubermann, and hundreds of others. Even Arturo Toscanini, notoriously reluctant to write testimonials, scribbled one on the back of a letter. Between 1916 and 1930 the Steinways had the greatest of the musicians, past and present, whose names were associated with theirs, portrayed by well-known painters for use in their advertisements. Some of the paintings are reproduced in this book.

Then came the crash of 1929, and the market for luxury goods was wiped out overnight. Like many companies, Steinway & Sons had to cut back severely beginning in 1931. Fortunately, they were able to hold most of their skilled staff together and succeeded in surviving. It was during this period that two of Steinway's most revolutionary modern inventions were developed: the diaphragmatic soundboard, which greatly enhances the tone of the smaller instruments, and improved key mounting, which made possible the famous accelerated action, with its highly sensitive response.

As if the depression were not bad enough, electronic recording and radio were now driving the player pianos off the market for good. Yet Steinway & Sons' salvation came in part from just this quarter. They knew better than to pit themselves against technical progress. Instead, encouraged by their own sales to schools and institutions and by radio's broadening influence on musical life, they sought and found customers among radio stations at home and abroad. As early as 1929, Steinway Hall had housed a broadcasting studio. By 1942, 180 pianos had been sold to NBC and CBS in New York alone and had proved their quality and sturdiness under the hard use and extreme temperature changes visited upon them in the studios.

Another important factor in the continuing existence of Steinway was the firm's long-standing interest in the development of small instruments, so farsightedly begun by Henry Ziegler in the early years of the century. The five-foot, one-inch "baby grand" and the 40-inch upright of the 1930s could be sold to people of modest means whose homes were small. As an investment, Stein-

way pianos of all sizes retained their high value; at the depth of the depression many of them brought 50 to 60 per cent of their list price at auction, whereas most household goods were bringing only 10 or 15 per cent.

In 1938 the firm presented a second grand piano, number 300,000, to the nation, to replace the instrument given in 1903. It stands in the East Room of the White House, where many concerts and receptions are held. For nearly half a century the firm, through its representatives Henry Junge and Alexander W. Greiner, has enjoyed the privilege of serving as unofficial musical adviser to the White House.

Steinway & Sons were not idle during the years of World War II, even though pianos were declared nonessential to the war effort. At the factories parts were built for the large troop-carrying gliders for the U.S. Army Air Force: wings, underbodies, and tail assemblies. At the same time, piano making did not come to a dead stop. Over 2,500 40-inch verticals were sold to the United States Government beginning in 1942—the famous field pianos, or G.I. Pianos, as they were frequently called. From Western Europe to New Guinea, from the tropics to the Arctic Circle, this sturdy little vertical proved its worth under almost incredible climatic handicaps. Of the 228 Steinway men in the services five gave their lives.

The years following the war brought a surprisingly quick recovery of some of the markets that had been hit hardest. The old Schanzenstrasse plant in Hamburg had been destroyed in 1943, but no sooner was the rubble-filled lot sold than a new unit was going up at the other Hamburg factory.

At the same time, television was opening up a wholly new dimension in the dissemination of music, and here, too, the Steinway is the standard piano in the studios.

On the day this book went to press, Steinway & Sons shipped their 341,862nd instrument, a Model "M" grand.

The first White House Steinway, built in 1903.

Royal appointments of Steinway & Sons, as shown on a
soundboard stencil, about 1903.

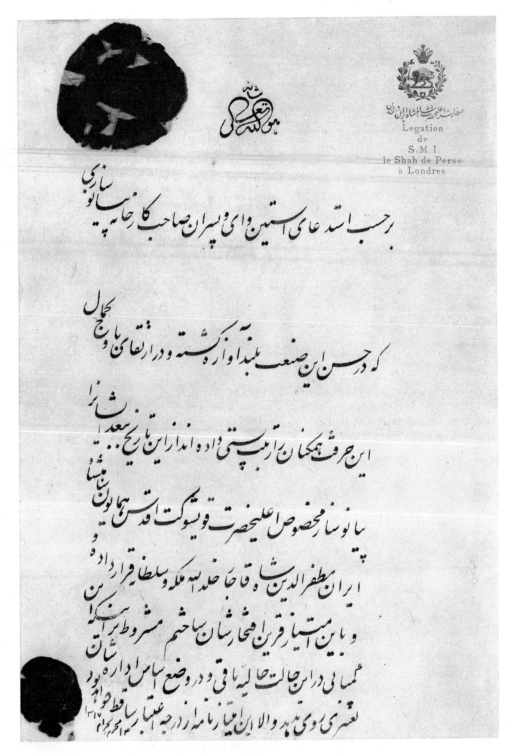

Appointment by the Shah of Persia, 1899.

"By the glory of God . . . The fame of the above firm is well known for the excellence and high merit in the manufacture of their pianos . . . Consequently, from this date on, His Majesty Muzaffar-ad-Din, Shah of the Qajar Dynasty, appoints the above firm as the especial manufacturers to the Court of Persia, provided the present excellence of this high art manufacture is maintained, otherwise this royal appointment will be abrogated."

By the turn of the century Steinways were sold on every
continent. Piano delivery in London, 1901 *(above)*, and
somewhere in India *(below)*.

In order that I may be sure myself that the workmen and carvers you have are capable of carrying out the design for the piano which I have made for Colonel Payne in the way I should like to have it done, I enclose you herewith a tracing showing a portion of the carving. Be kind enough to have this carved out of French walnut, and send it to me without touching it with oil or varnish of any kind. It must be carved out of the solid, although, of course, you can make the solid block of veneers, if you prefer. I will agree to pay for the cost of this, if you wish me to.

Yours truly,

Letter from Stanford White, 1897. Custom-made luxury pianos reached their greatest popularity about this time.

Luxury grand with painted panels, made for F. W. Woolworth in 1901.

Paderewski at the height of his fame, playing the Steinway
as he did in 1891. Caricature of unknown date.

Around 1900, the Steinway concert department gave up
artist management and began to concentrate on supplying
concert and rehearsal instruments for such artists as *(left
to right):* Leopold Godowsky, Josef Lhévinne, Fannie
Bloomfield-Zeisler, and Ferruccio Busoni.

Steinway owners and users among the composers *(left to right):* Giacomo Puccini, Gustav Mahler, Richard Strauss, and Edward Elgar.

Letter from Max Reger to the Steinway office in Hamburg, 1907. Then as now, Steinway's services to music often transcended the purely musical.

". . . Please tell the cigar dealer to send me IMMEDIATELY 30 (thirty) marks' worth *of little cigars* C.O.D. (EXACTLY *the same brand* as in the enclosed *tin box* . . .)"

Schanzenstrasse factory in Hamburg, with addition built
between 1909 and 1913.

Assembly plant at Ditmars Avenue, Long Island City,
after three stories had been added to the original building.
The transfer of manufacturing to Long Island, begun in
1871, was completed in 1910.

Material handling: Theodore Cassebeer, Long Island factory manager *(right)*, with Daniel Callahan, lumber-yard foreman, about 1925.

Charles H. Steinway (1857-1919), who became head of the firm in 1896, with the managing directors of the London and Hamburg branches, Edwin Eshelby *(left)* and Arthur von Holwede *(right)*, in 1906. The European units have always been branches of the New York State corporation, not foreign companies.

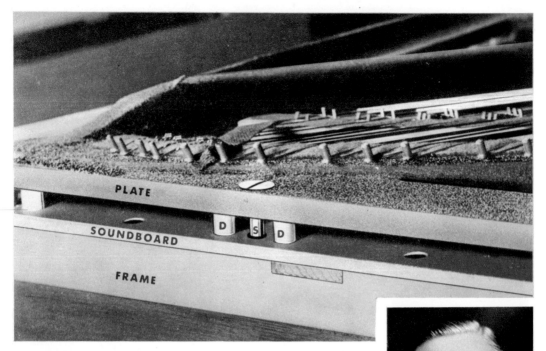

PLATE

SOUNDBOARD

FRAME

Acoustic dowel construction, invented by Henry Ziegler *(right)*, chief engineer after C. F. Theodore Steinway, in 1898.

The plate rests firmly on dowels (D) above the soundboard without touching it. At intervals, screws (S), running through oversize holes in the soundboard, attach the plate to the piano frame underneath. Before Ziegler's invention the plate was attached directly to the soundboard, hampering its vibrations.

Quality control, about 1900: break-testing machine in the office of Albert J. Menzl, Long Island factory superintendent.

IN HONOR OF THE MEN OF OUR HOUSE WHO HAVE ANSWERED THE CALL OF THEIR COUNTRY FOR MILITARY DUTY STEINWAY & SONS

FREDERICK A. VIETOR	RUDOLPH KOCH
HUBERT J. FISCHER	ELDON G. JOUBERT
WALTER J. MUELLER	HENRY C. PFAFF
OTTO GOEHL	WILLIAM BUSHMAN
EDWIN B. ORCUTT	GUSTAV NELSON
HENRY MILLER	LOUIS PARDON
HUGO KURBS, JR.	JOHN BELLI
JOHN KONDRATH	CHAS. SCHNEIDER
LOUIS OPOCHINSKY	JOSEPH BAGNASCO
FRANK McGILLIGET	FRANK GERDON
JOSEPH FIEDERLEIN	WILLIAM NULLE
WILLIAM DOERRIE	MICHAEL PISHITELLO
MURDOCK MACFARLANE	RAFAELE RICCIO
FRANK KESSLER	MAX FISCHER
KARL SCHUBERT	GEORGE STARKE
JOHN EICHENBRENNER	THOMAS IBBOTSON
LAWRENCE PORTER	FRED SCHNITZERLING
★ JOHN RICHARD	ROBERT SCHMITZ
JOHN NOLDE	PAUL EICHENBRENNER
DANIEL UTEMARK	PAUL MUNNICH
MAX PFUND	H. HORNUNG
F. RATHGEBER	★ A. BARTOLOMEO
A. SODERBERG	S. AYUSO
WILLIAM F. EVERTSBERG	★ JOSEPH WENZ
CHARLES H. KIEFER	F. J. CRONIN
A. RUDOLPH	C. EBERSOLD
H. HACKERT	S. STREITHORST
C. ROECKELL	W. LINDSTEDT
F. H. EDWARDS	W. HUPFER
A. MOSS	E. von HONE
C. DRASCHE	I. W. HOBEIN
C. A. ZIEGLER	

"THE RIGHT IS MORE PRECIOUS THAN PEACE, WE SHALL FIGHT FOR THE THINGS WHICH WE HAVE ALWA CARRIED NEAREST OUR HEARTS TO SUCH A TASK WE DEDICATE OUR LIVES"

Steinway in the First World War: 63 men from the firm were in service; three gave their lives. Two of the Steinway family were servicemen: Charles F. M. Steinway *(left)* and Frederick A. Vietor.

Frederick T. Steinway (1860-1927), president of Steinway & Sons, 1919-1927.

The heyday of the player piano: advertising illustration of 1924, showing the recess above the keyboard, where the perforated rolls that actuated the keys were inserted. Many Steinway pianos were equipped with player mechanisms by the Aeolian Company of America.

West 57th Street, New York, in 1925. The new Steinway
Hall, completed in that year, is number 109.

Interior of new Steinway Hall, New York. *Below:* Studio 1 of Radio Station WABC, in Steinway Hall, 1929.

Expansion in Europe: The new Steinway Hall in London.
1 and 2, St. George Street, W. 1, opened in 1925.

Delivery of a concert instrument, Nagpur, India, 1923.
Helena Morsztyn, pianist, at right.

Noted Steinway pianists of the years between the wars *(left to right):* Ignaz Friedman, Ossip Gabrilowitsch, Rudolph Ganz, and Mischa Levitzki.

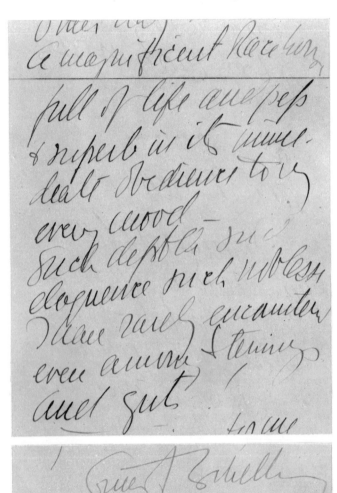

Letter from Ernest Schelling to Theodore E. Steinway, 1928, about an instrument he played in a recital.

". . . A magnificent Race horse full of life and pep & superb in its immediate obedience to my every mood. Such depth such eloquence such noblesse I have rarely encountered even among Steinways. *And guts . . .*"

Serge Rachmaninoff, who came to the United States after
the Russian Revolution, here shown at the Steinway in
rehearsal with Eugene Ormandy *(right)*, 1940.

Four popular musicians who used the Steinway *(left to
right):* Victor Herbert, John McCormack, Al Jolson, and
George Gershwin.

Theodore E. Steinway (b. 1883), president of the firm since 1927.

One of 14 instruments, bought by the Australian Broadcasting Corporation, being shipped from Hamburg in the early 1930s. William R. Steinway, European general manager, supervises the loading.

Above: The Steinway's status as the standard studio piano for radio broadcasting dates from the 1930s, when the expansion of radio was offering a much needed new market. *Below:* Steinway grand in use during a CBS broadcast by Will Osborne and his orchestra, 1934.

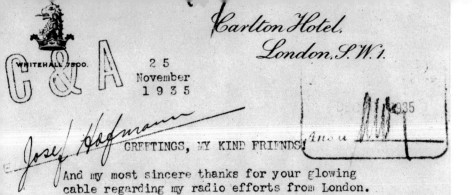

Carlton Hotel.
London, S.W.1.

C & A
WHITEHALL 7500.

2 5
November
1935

GREETINGS, MY KIND FRIENDS!

And my most sincere thanks for your glowing
cable regarding my radio efforts from London.

Such a broadcast is an interesting experience, but
would be, I dare say, a lot easier if one did not
know until AFTER the broadcast, the extent of the
hook-up! North America was not the only distant
country to which the Queen's Hall concert on the 6th
inst. was relayed. Cables even from South Africa
assured me that it was clearly heard there, also.

An extraordinary world we are living in - and it
appears that it is not only the government budget
that goes into unlimited figures - but the radio
audiences as well!

Betty and I look forward to the time when I have
finished distributing my musical goods about europe -
and we will see you all again.

Our warm greetings to all at Steinway Hall and again
my thanks for the thoughtful message.

                    Most sincerely,

                    Josef Hofmann

Josef Hofmann, shown below at the piano built by Henry
Engelhard Steinway about 1836, tells about the first concert he played on a transatlantic radio hookup, 1935.

Rim of a five-foot, one-inch grand, a size first built in 1936, next to the rim of a nine-foot concert grand. The development of the smallest grand pianos, begun by Henry Ziegler as early as 1910, helped the Steinways survive the depression.

Accelerated action, invented, 1931-1936, by Frederick A. Vietor.

Instant reply to the touch of the finger is made possible by balancing keys on a rounded instead of a square fulcrum (A), and by minute regulation of lead weights inside the key (B).

Fritz Kreisler's 1888 debut under Steinway auspices led to a continuing friendship with the firm. Here, in the 1940s, he again rehearses the Mendelssohn concerto, which he played at his debut.

Friends of the Steinway in the 1920s and 1930s: Olga Samaroff, Ernestine Schumann-Heink, Albert Spalding, Frederick Stock. Walter Damrosch (*right*) once wrote of his piano: "I have nailed it to the floor in order that you may never be able to take it away again."

The second White House Steinway, number 300,000, made in 1938. For many years Steinway & Sons have assisted in planning musical entertainment at the White House.

The G.I. Field Piano. Over 2,500 have been built since 1942.

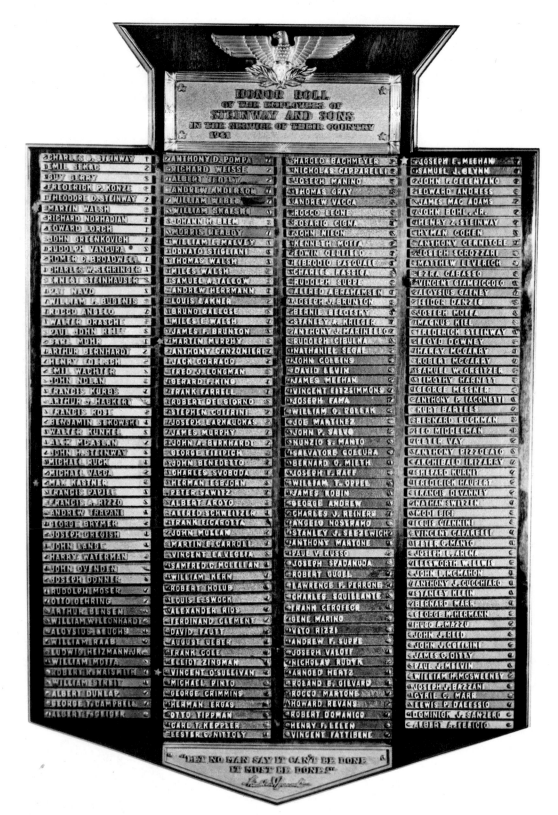

Two hundred twenty-eight of the company's men
were in the Second World War; all but five came back.

Five Steinway sons saw service *(left to right):* Theodore
D., Charles G., Henry Z., John H., and Frederick.

Main components of gliders were made at the Steinway
factories during the Second World War. Piano manufacture was limited to the G.I. model in July, 1942.

Helen gave me a fine idea last night which I pass on to you, hoping you can tell me how to push it over. She said that Ernest ought to be the first pianist to play for television, and we ought to see about it right away while his fingers are still nimble. At the Juilliard summer session he is giving this summer his well known series of historical recitals. There are plenty of people who'd enjoy watching his technique as well as listening to the results, and television is the ideal medium. What do you think?

Should I speak to Judson or to Sarnoff? I'd like to arrange it so that Ernest would have the pleasure of a slight surprise in receiving the invitation.

Faithfully always

John Erskine

Television expanded suddenly in 1946. Although John Erskine's plan to have Ernest Hutcheson give the first televised piano recital did not materialize, many fine programs have since been seen and heard by millions.

The Steinway piano on television is not always used for serious music: it has been through such adventures as this telecast at NBC in 1950, with Jimmy Durante.

IN TUNE WITH THE FUTURE

In the scale room at the Ditmars Avenue factory, plans
for future Steinways are drawn up full size under the
guidance of Theodore D. Steinway (*center*).

IN TUNE WITH THE FUTURE

*There is nothing better, than that a man should rejoice
in his own works, for that is his portion.*

ECCLESIASTES

If Henry Engelhard Steinway should revisit the firm's factories today, he would feel quite at home. There are, of course, many differences. Production is on a greatly enlarged scale. Also, the Steinway piano of today is a vast improvement over the instrument of a hundred years ago, both in point of design and technique. At the same time, the founder would see that his insistence on the importance of expert craftsmanship still guides his descendants in their work.

He would find his grandchildren and great-grandchildren firmly established in the city to which he came a century ago— working in the factories and offices, side by side with craftsmen whose fathers and grandfathers, in many cases, worked there before them. And he would find a namesake in the fifth generation of the family, for the youngest member living at the time of this centennial is his great-great-grandson Henry Engelhard Steinway.

The days of William Steinway's pioneering in such civic developments as streetcar lines, ferry services, the Steinway fire department, school, library, and kindergarten have gone; these functions are now filled by municipal authority. Likewise, actual management of concert artists is no longer a role

of the company, and Steinway Hall, which for nearly a quarter of a century was the scene of many of New York's principal musical events, has long since been superseded by Carnegie Hall. Thus the family and the firm now are able to devote their energies more fully to the piano which is the world's standard of excellence and to their consequent responsibilities as friends of artists in this country and abroad and as advisers, directly and through their many dealers, of music lovers in all walks of life.

The craftsmanship which characterized the work of the founder is still practiced by his descendants. Mass production, the rule in many industries, cannot be applied to the making of fine pianos. The Steinway plant, therefore, is one-third modern factory and two-thirds a craftsman's shop. Not that the firm is reluctant to use machinery as such (power-driven tools were first installed nearly a century ago), but the art of piano making puts definite limits to mechanization; it is still basically a hand operation.

Some of the qualities that make a fine instrument, notably richness of tone and balance of volume, are principally matters of taste and judgment, not of measurement and formula. In the Steinway factories dampers and hammers, for example, are regulated by hand and tested by the trained ear of the experienced worker. Although research in methods and machinery is always going on, it seems probable that tasks like these will always require hand work for best results.

From the G.I. vertical to the nine-foot concert grand, every Steinway piano is built from the same materials and with the same care. The wood for soundboards, rims, and countless other wooden parts is all selected from the same lumber piles; the wire for strings from the same metal stocks—for grand pianos, spinets, and studio verticals. One month a Steinway craftsman may be working on a hand-carved Louis XV grand— another month on a plain-cased vertical. Both instruments receive the same insistence on perfection, the same careful testing and adjustment.

Even though piano making cannot be a mass production industry, it is dependent on continuous scientific research and experimentation. To the qualities which make the piano the basic musical instrument—its great range, its flexibility, its precision, and its tonal variety—Steinway & Sons have made notable contributions. Among the more recent are the principle of accelerated action which, through its extreme sensitivity and rapid response, is more than a match for the dexterity of the virtuoso, and the patented diaphragmatic soundboard of hand-picked spruce, which makes possible "big piano" tone even in the smaller instruments.

A mechanism so complex, containing nearly 12,000 individual parts, offers almost endless avenues of investigation. New materials and methods of manufacture are under constant scrutiny by Steinway's research staff. Electronic gluing methods and new surfaces for piano keys are among the fields currently being explored. This continuous research throughout the years has resulted in an instrument that is widely recognized as the leading piano throughout the world.

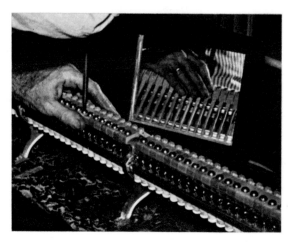

Detail of action assembly.

As musicians travel through the country and around the world, the facilities of the house of Steinway are always at their service. In addition to the stock of 130 concert pianos in Steinway Hall in New York, where many musicians come to choose their instruments, almost 400 concert grands are kept in stock with dealers all over the country, and many more abroad. An artist on tour can always be sure that a Steinway will be waiting for him at his next port of call. An unusual instance of the firm's service to musicians was the solution of Artur Rubinstein's predicament. Once he found himself in Buenos Aires without his own piano, which was on board a ship unable to dock on account of a strike. He wired Alexander W. Greiner, the firm's concert artist manager, at Steinway Hall in New York, who promptly shipped by air another concert grand, which he knew Rubinstein would like.

In the United States alone there are 152 franchised dealers and over 300 outlets— many of them linked with Steinway for 50 years or more. All of them are helping to celebrate the firm's hundredth birthday. Among the oldest are the Siegling Music House in Charleston, South Carolina, since the late sixties; Lyon & Healy in Chicago, since the early seventies; and the Jenkins Music Company in Kansas City, Missouri, which this year celebrates its own 75th anniversary and, at the same time, three generations of dealing with three generations of the Steinway family.

The Steinway dealers' thorough knowledge of the product which they sell compels, too, a feeling of responsibility toward the service of music in their own communities. They stand ready to provide instruments for artists, they guide families in the choice of appropriate instruments for their homes, and they offer authorized tuning and repair service. Their advice in such matters is not based on guesswork but on experience gained under the guidance of the Steinway sales manager, Roman de Majewski; they are regular and frequent visitors at the factories in Long Island City.

Many dealers know families that have had the Steinway habit over the years. Perhaps a cherished instrument has served two generations or more; perhaps each child eventually bought a Steinway for his home—thus the tradition continues. In such families the "Instrument of the Immortals" is the instrument of little children playing their first scales, of men and women tired from the day's work who relax with music, of family groups gathered for carol singing at Christmas; it is a part of the home.

To the Steinways, the artists who play their instruments have always been of great importance, and the present Steinway Hall on West 57th Street in New York is a rendezvous for the many friends of the firm. There the private studios may be visited by Leopold Stokowski, looking for a place to rehearse a concerto; or by Albert Einstein, who may while away an hour there with his violin between trains. Hardly a day goes by that a musician, professional or amateur, does not drop in to try a new piano, talk over developments in the concert field, or simply pass the time of day. The fact that music lovers in all walks of life know the Steinway and prefer it to others is the strongest compulsion for the firm to continue that extra effort needed to make the best piano.

The founder of the House of Steinway a century ago felt keenly his debt to music; it was a debt that made him look ceaselessly for ways of improving the piano. Under him and his children, a great business grew up and flourished in the stimulating climate of a new and vigorous nation, giving livelihood to thousands of workers and producing the instrument which to many people has come to mean *the* piano. Today, working in their factories and offices, his grandchildren and great-grandchildren are still prompted by Henry Engelhard Steinway's devotion to craftsmanship and his deep sense of obligation to music. The Steinways of future generations will see to it that this tradition lives on—that Steinway's second century of service to music is as fruitful as the first.

Plaque commemorating Steinway's centenary, 1953.

The Steinway plant in Long Island City today: parts
manufacture at Riker Avenue *(above)*; assembly plant at
Ditmars Avenue *(below)*.

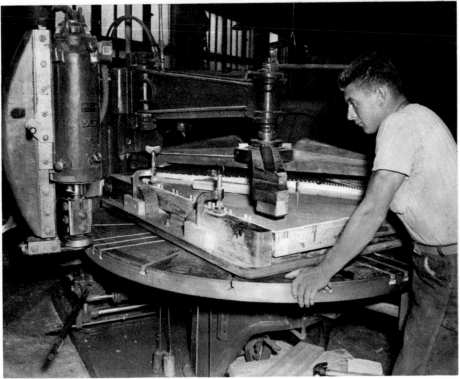

Mechanical equipment is used in gluing up the backs of
vertical pianos *(above)*. Modern machinery is also used in
such woodworking operations as shaping *(below)*.

Like most of the woodworking, turning of legs *(left)* is done on a machine by skilled hands.

Stringing *(below)*, although involving assembly of machined parts, is itself a hand operation.

Above: The action, embracing keys, hammers, and intervening parts, contains a majority of the 12,000 pieces in the piano, mostly tiny bits of wood and felt. *Below:* The soundboard of a concert grand receives the finishing touch.

Decorative carving of cases and legs for custom-made
pianos calls for the greatest skill and care.

Damper regulation *(above)* to attain evenness of performance requires a high degree of technical competence.
"Voicing" the piano *(below)*—that is, treating the hammers
to ensure proper tone quality—depends largely on the ear
and judgment of the regulator.

HOROWITZ uses the Steinway exclusively, as do virtually all the great artists today: Anderson, Brailowsky, Casadesus, First Piano Quartet, Heifetz, Hess, Jonas, Kapell, Kurtz, Landowska, Muench, Artur Rubinstein, Hazel Scott, Serkin, Vronsky & Babin, Walter, and many, many more. . . . Over 1000 music schools and music departments of leading colleges use the Steinway. . . . The exquisite Vertical illustrated above is the Hepplewhite . . . . For the name of your local Steinway representative, consult your classified telephone directory.

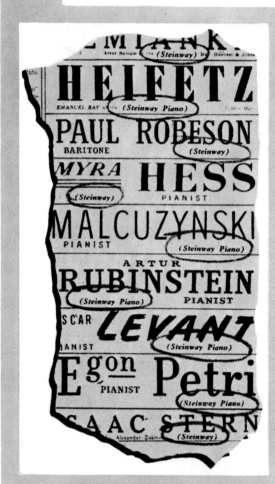

Rachmaninoff created enduring music at the Steinway, as did Paderewski, Berlioz, Gounod. Today virtually every great artist uses the Steinway: Brailowsky, Casadesus, Gorodnitzki, Hofmann, Horowitz, Kapell, List, Maynor, Menuhin, Reiner, Artur Rubinstein, Rodzinski, Serkin, Wallenstein, Whittemore & Lowe, Zaremba, and many more. . . . In the New York area alone, the Steinway is used in more than 90% of concerts and recitals. . . . For name of your nearest Steinway representative, consult your local classified telephone directory.

The Steinway continues today, as it has in the past, to be the favorite piano of many noted musicians. Excerpts from magazine advertisements, 1945-1948. (Names of Steinway artists appear on page 107ff.)

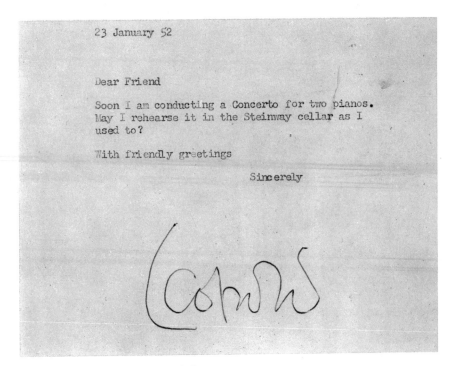

23 January 52

Dear Friend

Soon I am conducting a Concerto for two pianos.
May I rehearse it in the Steinway cellar as I
used to?

With friendly greetings

Sincerely

The lifetime friendship of musicians is one of the piano
maker's most prized rewards. Letter from Leopold Stokowski to Theodore E. Steinway, 1952.

Transportation of a piano by air from New York to Buenos
Aires for a concert by Artur Rubinstein, 1947. The first
instance of a grand piano's being flown to a concert.

"Steinway piano is really tops,
A dandy grand for classical or pops.
Keeps in tune much longer, too.
Steinway piano is the make for you."

Steinway Hall showroom: Cartoon by Whitney Darrow, Jr., *The New Yorker*, 1953.

Directors of Steinway & Sons, 1953. *Seated, left to right:*
Frederick J. Ziegler, Jerome F. Murphy, Theodore E.
Steinway, and William R. Steinway. *Standing:* Henry Z.
Steinway, Edwin B. Orcutt, and Roman de Majewski.

Many Steinway dealers can look back on long years of
association with the firm. Roman de Majewski, Steinway
sales manager, with Paul W. Jenkins, at the celebration
of the 75th anniversary of the Jenkins Music Company.

E. D. Horwood *(left)* and Theodor Ehrlich *(right)*, the heads of the firm's London and Hamburg units, with Theodore E. Steinway, 1953.

Three generations of Steinways, 1953.

Front row, left to right: William T. (b. 1946); Theodore E. (b. 1883), holding Robert C. (b. 1952); Frederick E. (b. 1951); William R. (b. 1881), holding Henry E. (b. 1952); Daniel K. (b. 1948). *Back row:* Frederick (b. 1921); John H. (b. 1917); Henry Z. (b. 1915); Theodore D. (b. 1914); Charles F. M. (b. 1892); Charles G. (b. 1914).

STEINWAY ARTISTS

Wanda Landowska

Ronald Hodges

Skitch Henderson

Bruce Simonds

Ian Swartenberg

Eugene Istomin

Victor de Sabata

Isaac Stern

Claudette Sorel

Byron Janis

Beveridge Webster

Vladimir Sokolow

Samuel Sorin

Kronsky and Babin

Rosalyn Tureck

Zadel Skolovsky

Leo Smit

Elton Jones

Arthur Rubinstein

William Kapell

Jeanne Mitchell

Erich Itor Kahn

Leonid Hambro

Maurice Abravanel

Reginald Stewart

Mack Harrell

Gary Graffman

Rudolf Serkin

[signature]

Arthur Ferrante

Louis Teicher

Yehudi Menuhin

Nadia Reisenberg

[signature]

Wheeler Beckett

H. Arthur Brown

Egon Petri

James Friskin

German Todaro

[signature]

Jean Sibelius

Sidney Sukoenig

N. Milstein

[signature]

Robert Fizdale

Myra Hess

Michael Rabin

Sylvia Zaremba

Leopold Mannes

Lawrence Tibbett

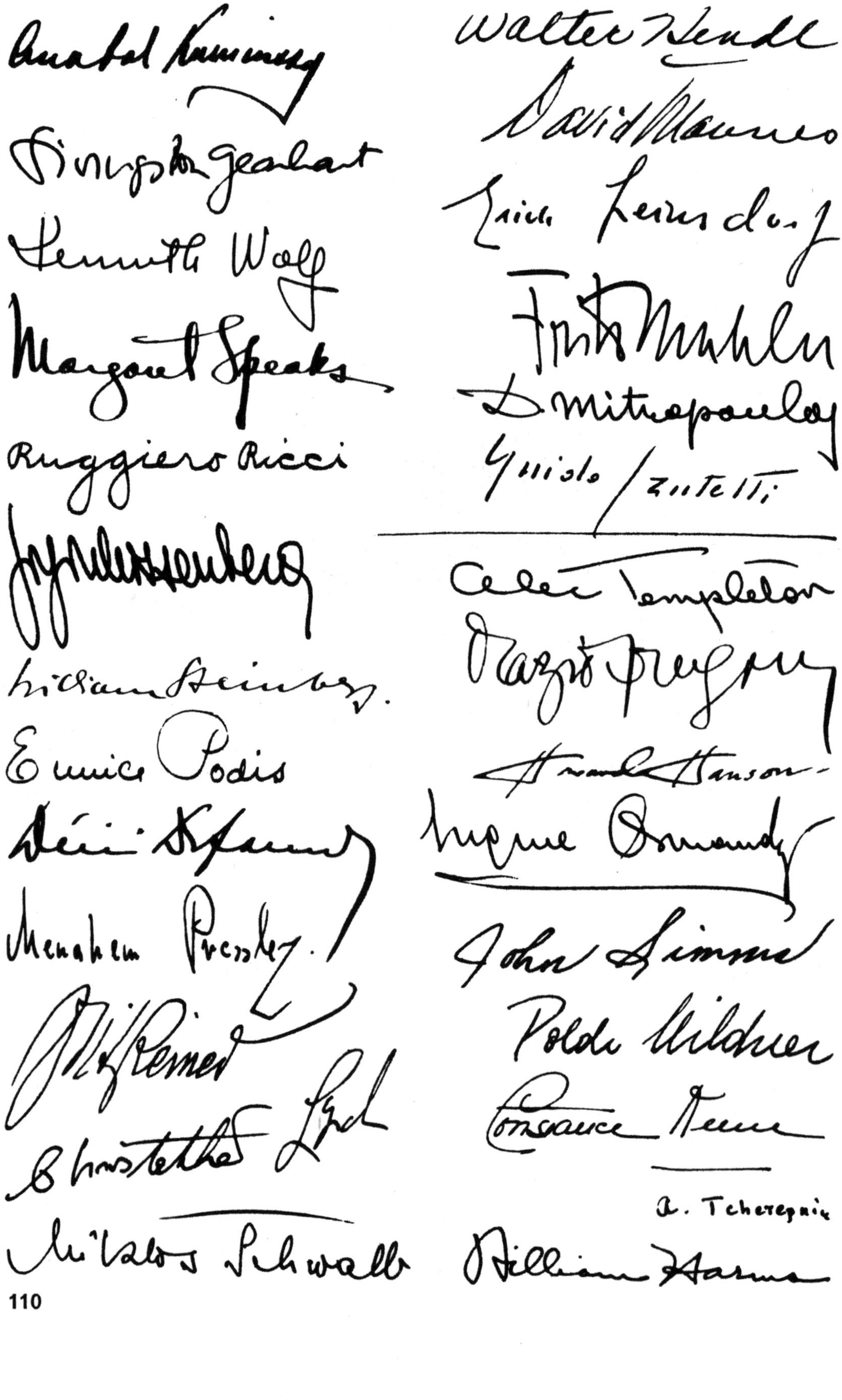
Ruggiero Ricci
Eunice Podis
Alec Templeton
John Simms
A. Tcherepnin

Jerome Rappaport
L. Saminsky
Patricia Travers
Bruno Walter
Ernst Hoffman.
Julius Katchen
Henri Temianka

Lélia Gousseau

Reah Sadowsky

Manfred Malkin

A. Brailowsky

Blanche Thebom

Gina Bachauer

Alexander Borovsky

Grant Johannesen

Raya Garbousova

Lari Dua

Maryla Jonas

Grace Tracey

Andor Foldes

Ole Windingstad

Mona Bates

Aurora Mauro-Cottone

Guy Maier

Toena and Louise Leschin

Hadley Smedbvorst

Wilh. Grm

Dorothy Munger

Georges Enesco

Paul Badura-Skoda

John Powell

Ellen Ballou

Ginnias Morales Pinto

Fritz Kreisler

Mieczyslaw Munz

Ethel Bartlett & Rae Robertson

[Page of handwritten signatures of Steinway Artists, 1953]

Luisa M. Stojowska

Henri Deering

Veronica Mimoso

Sascha Gorodnitzki

Mischa Elman

Sidney Foster

Helena Morsztyn

Frank Glazer

Friedrich Gulda

Hazel Scott

Seymour Lipkin

Frank Glazer

Hortense Monath

Rudolph Ganz

Isabelle Vengerova

Katherine Bacon

Raymond Lewenthal

Samuel Dushkin

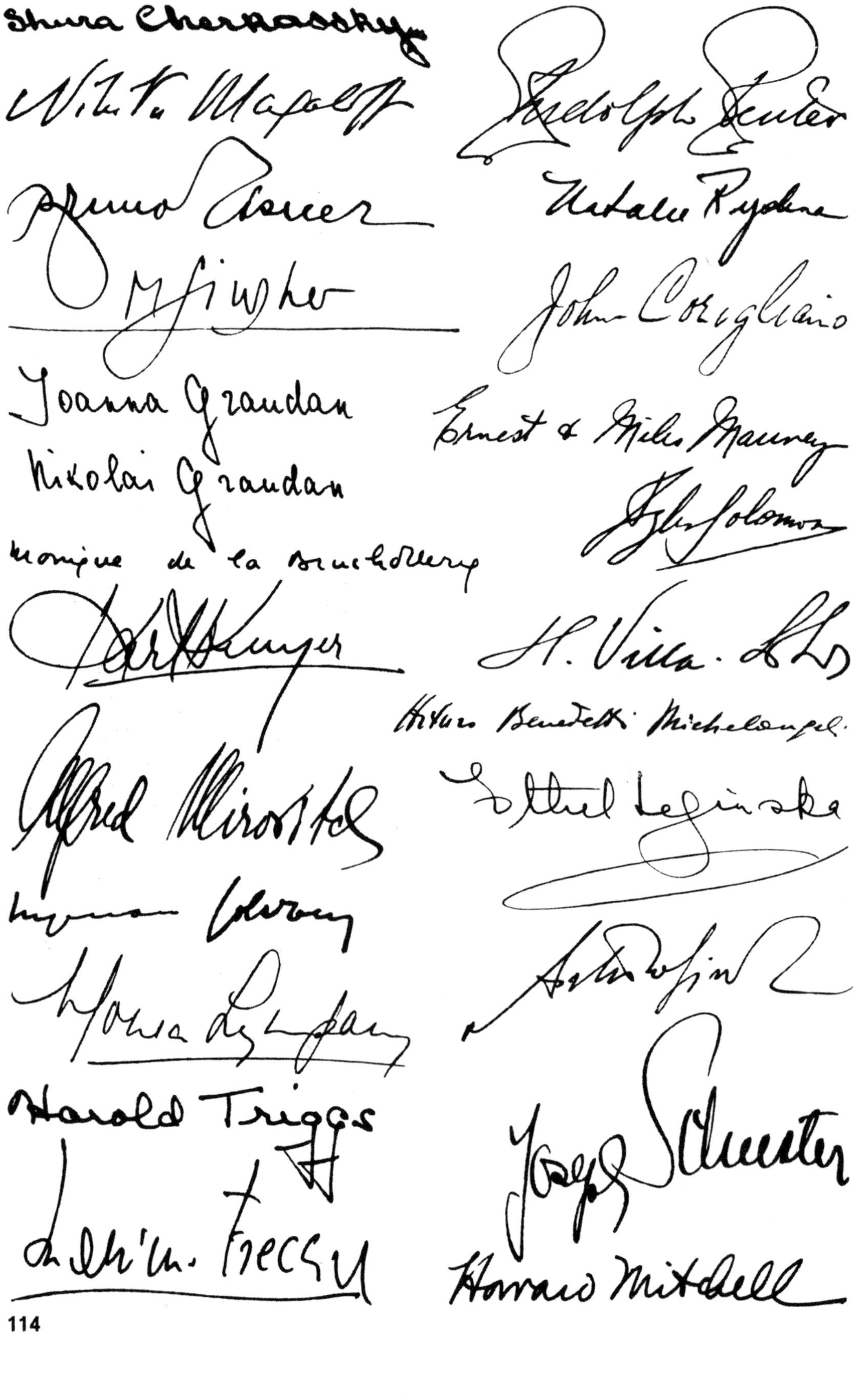

[Page of handwritten signatures of Steinway artists, including:]

Clifford Curzon
Abram Chasins
Josef Hofmann

Leonard Rose
Maryan Filar

David Gibson

Frank Golomia (?)
Grace Castagnetta
B. Segall

Walter Golde
Marian Anderson
William Masselos

Jean Graham
Solomon
Henry Fleming (?)
John Leer(?) Thomas
James de la Fuente
I. Philipp
George Copeland
Jacob Lateiner
Ania Dorfmann
Sylvia Rabinof
Carl Friedberg
Donald Vail Allen
Tomas Cramer (?)
Leon Fleisher

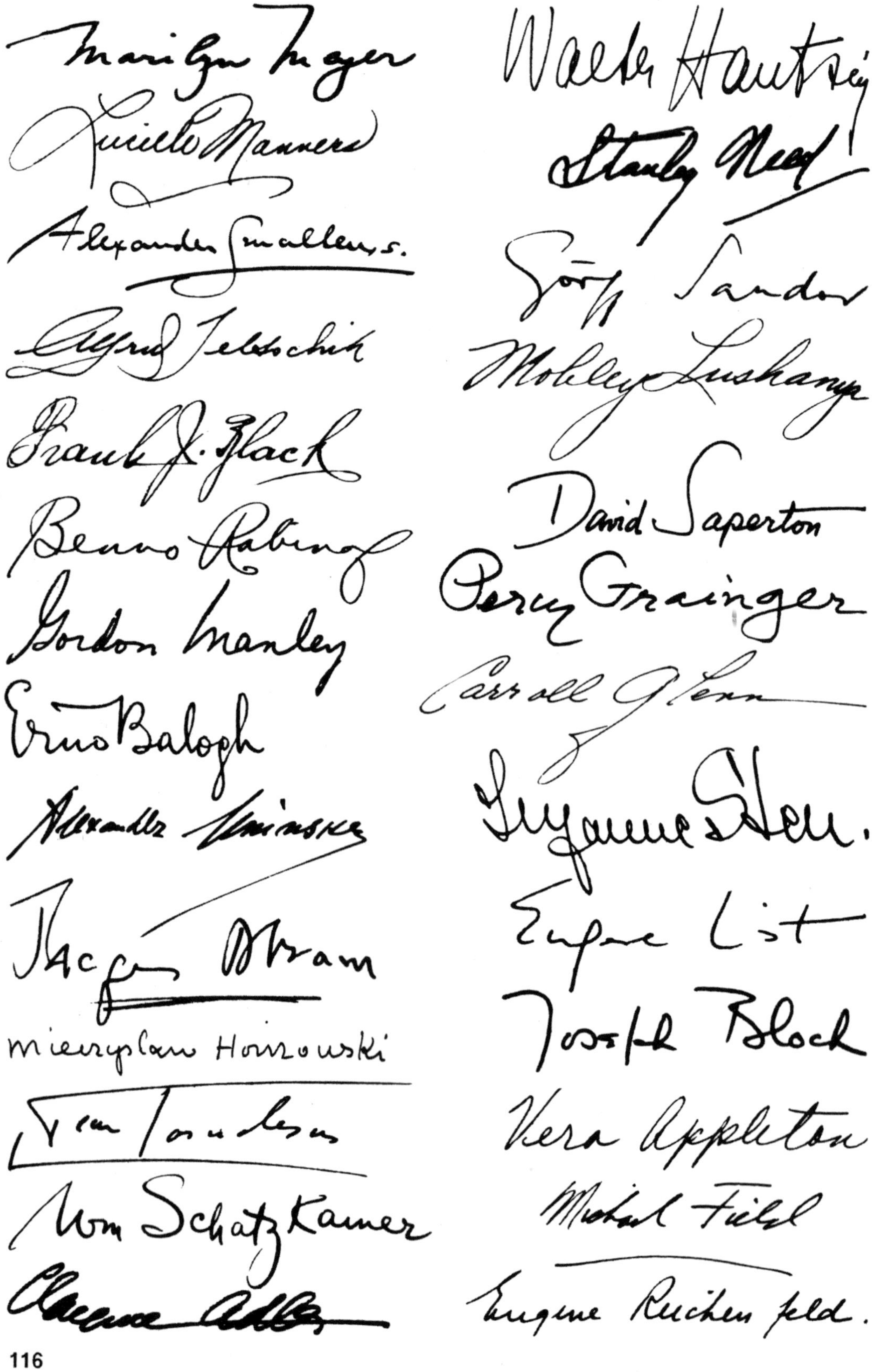
Walter Hautzig
Stanley Need
Frank J. Black
David Saperton
Benno Rabinof
Percy Grainger
Gordon Manley
Erno Balogh
Joseph Block
Vera Appleton

Max Reger

Dr. H. v. Helmholtz

Serge Prokofieff

Francis Alda

George Gershwin

Ant. Rubinstein

Sigismund Stojowski

Vict. Herbert

Ch. Gounod

Prof. Ferruccio B. Busoni

Frederick A. Stock

Hector Berlioz.

Les Barrère

Ignaz Friedman

Henry Hadley.

Schumann Heink

Liszt

Enrico Caruso

Adelina Patti

Richard Wagner.

Emma Calvé.

Walter Damrosch

Edward MacDowell

ACKNOWLEDGMENTS AND SOURCES

In the preparation of this book, helpful information and material have been received from Rodman Gilder, Gordon Grant, Adrian Siegel, Frank O. Braynard of the American Merchant Marine Institute, Inc., and Miss May Davenport Seymour of the Museum of the City of New York, as well as from the staff of The New York Public Library and that of The New-York Historical Society. To all of them, sincere thanks.

The list below gives the origins of all illustrations obtained through the courtesy of their owners or reproduced from previous publications. Illustrations not listed were taken from original pictures or documents in the possession of Steinway & Sons.

Page

15. S. S. "Helene Sloman": From a painting in the possession of Robert M. Sloman, Jr.; photograph courtesy of Dr. K. J. Sattelmair.

16. Jenny Lind: Engraving by Johnson, Fry & Company.
Castle Garden: Lithograph by George W. Lewis, about 1852.

18. Square piano: Steinway catalogue, 1865.

19. Crystal Palace: *Gleason's Pictorial Drawing-Room Companion*, January 1, 1853.

20. Diagram of overstrung square piano: Steinway catalogue, 1876.
Diagram of overstrung grand: Steinway prospectus, 1888.

21. Advertisement: *Frank Leslie's Illustrated Newspaper*, May 26, 1860.

22. Factory: *Leslie's*, September 22, 1860.

23. Opening reception: *ibid.*
Sawing and planing room: *Leslie's*, May 28, 1864.

24. Steinway Hall: *Leslie's*, May 28, 1864.

25. Inaugural procession: *Leslie's*, March 25, 1865.

26. Ticket queue for Dickens reading: *Leslie's*, December 28, 1867.
Vienna Lady Orchestra: *Leslie's*, September 30, 1871.

27. Communists: *Daily Graphic*, New York, October 25, 1877.
Demonstration of music transmission: *Leslie's*, April 21, 1877.

28. Sales room: *Leslie's*, May 28, 1864.

30. Grand piano of 1876: Steinway catalogue, 1876.

34. Paderewski advertisement: *New York Times*, November 17, 1891.

35. Cupola frame: Steinway prospectus, 1888.

36. Duplex scale diagram: *ibid.*
Upright: *ibid.*, insert.

37. Rim-bending screws: U. S. Patent 229,198, June 22, 1880.

38. Tweed Ring cartoon: *Harper's Weekly*, Supplement, November 11, 1871.

40. Plan for subway station: New York City Rapid Transit Commissioners' Board, Report, 1891, exhibit 12.

41. Ferryboat: The New-York Historical Society, Murdock Collection.
Motor car: Daimler Motor Company catalogue, 1896.

42. Map: J. S. Kelsey, *History of Long Island City, N. Y.* (Long Island City, Long Island Star Publishing Company, 1896), p. 44.

43. Riker Avenue factory: Steinway prospectus, 1881.

44. Library: Kelsey, *op. cit.*, p. 48.

46. Cartoon: *Le Charivari*, 1867.

47. Machinery Hall: *The United States International Exhibition: The organization, the work proposed, the work already done* (Philadelphia, 1875), p. 59.

ACKNOWLEDGMENTS AND SOURCES

Page

47. Steinway exhibit: *Daily Graphic*, December 29, 1876.

51. Edison: Thomas Alva Edison Foundation.

52. Patti: Academy of Music, New York, program, November 29, 1886.

53. Rubinstein: Lithograph by Georg Engelbach.

54. Caricature: Photograph (from original wash drawing) in the possession of Steinway & Sons.

55. Seidl: Anton Seidl, editor, *The Music of the Modern World* (New York, D. Appleton & Company, 1895), frontispiece.

56. Essipova: *Gazeta musical*, Lisbon, June 15, 1884.
Joseffy: Postcard photograph in The New York Public Library, Picture Collection.

57. Tretbar: *Freund's Music and Drama*, Supplement, November 8, 1890.

58. Music Festival advertisement: *New York Times*, May 9, 1891.

58. Tchaikovsky: Postcard photograph in The New York Public Library, Picture Collection.

59. Paderewski: *Town Topics*, Supplement, January 30, 1896.
Review: *New York Tribune*, November 18, 1891.

70. Paderewski cartoon: Newspaper clipping in The New York Public Library, Picture Collection; source not identified.
Godowsky: Photograph in The New York Public Library, Music Division.

76. Player piano: Advertisement for Aeolian Duo-Art pianos, *Vanity Fair*, March 1924.

78. Studio: Columbia Broadcasting System.

81. Rachmaninoff: Adrian Siegel.
Jolson: Warner Bros. Pictures, Inc.

83. Broadcast: Columbia Broadcasting System.

86. Kreisler: Adrian Siegel.

87. G. I. piano: U. S. Army Signal Corps.

90. Durante: National Broadcasting Company.

104. Cartoon: *The New Yorker*, March 28, 1953.

Composition by The Composing Room, Inc.
Printing by Photogravure and Color Company
Binding by Russell-Rutter Company, Inc.
Design and supervision of production
      by Appleton, Parsons & Company, Inc.

New York, August 1953